#TWEETSTORMS

©2019 Michael Bournazian
Published by Flowerpublishing
ISBN 978-1-927914-93-9

All rights reserved. No part of this book may be reproduced, stored in a retrieval system or transmitted in any form or by any means without the prior permission of the publisher or author, except by reviewer who may quote brief passages for a review to be printed in a magazine, journal and newspaper.

FLOWERPUBLISHING

MONTREAL, CANADA

WWW.FLOWERPUBLISH.COM

Acknowledgements

Mom and Dad
MaryAnn Hayatian
Etc.

Photo Credits

Michael Bournazian
   Front Cover Photo, Author Photo, Selfie Nation, The Blue And The Brown, That Turning Point, Live In Peace, Pay Your Way To Happiness, Border Wall, Justice Does Not Age, Raving Nostomaniac, King Patrick

Angela Bhattachargee and Yotanka Coicou
   Back Cover Photo

Lorri St. Germain
   Cattitude

Dedication

To Mom and Dad (Ma and Ba)

CONTENTS

MAIN PROGRAM

An Explanation Please, Part 1
-18/19-

An Explanation Please, Part 2
- 20/21-

The Day After
- 22/23-

Golden Silence
- 24/25-

Selfie Nation
- 26/27-

The Big Picture, Part 1
-28/29-

Pissing Contest
-30/31-

The Broken Windows
-32/33-

Puerto Rico
-34/35-

The Blue And The Brown
-36/37-

Take A Knee
-38/39-

To Fallen Non-Friends
-40/41-

Intelligence Deficient
-42/43-

G.E.D.
-44/45-

That Turning Point
-46/47-

Rich Celebrity Rape Theory
-48/49-

Thoughts and Prayers
-50/51-

Costume Party In Amurca
-52/53-

Bonjour-Hi
-54/55-

Sober Moral High Ground
-56/57-

Niggard Is A Word
-58/59-

Blind Faith
-60/61-

Live In Peace
-62/63-

Pay Your Way To Happiness
-64/65-

The Big Picture, Part 2
-66/67-

Reality's Helping Hand
-68/69-

SingleMinded
-70/71-

#MeBecomingScaredToPraise
-72/73-

One Year In
-74/75-

First In Everything
-76/77-

Kill All Double Standards
-78/79-

Defame & Scold For Profit
-80/81-

Give Them The Brains,
Not The Guns
-82/83-

Distraction Warfare
-84/85-

Border Wall
-86/87-

LikeBlooded
-88/89-

Justice Does Not Age
-90/91-

The 25th
-92/93-

Restless Night
-94/95-

The Secrets Of Life
-96/97-

AntiSocial Media
-98/99-

Psycho The Rapist
-100/101-

Coat Of Harms
-102/103-

Entropy Monger
-104/105-

Raving Nostomaniac
-106/107-

OUTTWEETS

Haiku For Eric Stern
-110/111-

Cattitude
- 112/113-

King Patrick
- 114/115-

MAIN PROGRAM

#140

Is that all you can give?
Using big words too hard?
Being compassionate too hard?
Not being a racist too hard?
What say you POTUS?
Little

TWEET STORMS An Explanation Please, Part 1
@WhereDidThisIdeaComeFrom?

Pretty simple actually. I wrote a poem in the last book called #140, which was a tweet about Bitch Trump. Figured that if he could get by on

5:45 PM - 10 October 2017

TWEET STORMS An Explanation Please, Part 2
@GoOn

tweets alone, then surely I can. And mine would be way more intelligent. Well, anybody's would be, right? So enjoy some tweet poems <=140.

5:46 PM 10 October 2017

TWEET STORMS   **The Day After**   @WhatThe...

Fuck! Fuck! Fuck! Fuck! Fuck! Fuck! Fuck! Fuck! Fuck! Fuck! Fuck! Fuck! Fuck! Fuck! Fuck! Fuck! Fuckity Fuck Fuck! Fuck! Fuck! Off to work?!

5:00 AM - 9 November 2016

TWEET STORMS Golden Silence
@ZenMoment

A precious time in one's life
When the picture says everything
When you need less than 140
When all minds think the same way
Size it up

3:55 PM - 20 January 2017

TWEET STORMS   Selfie Nation
@NoOneCaresAboutEveryFuckingDetail

Some will sacrifice their hand
Or part of their arm
Or get slick and give the full picture
Tell me how you matter
So that I feel less worthy

4:55 PM - 9 October 2017

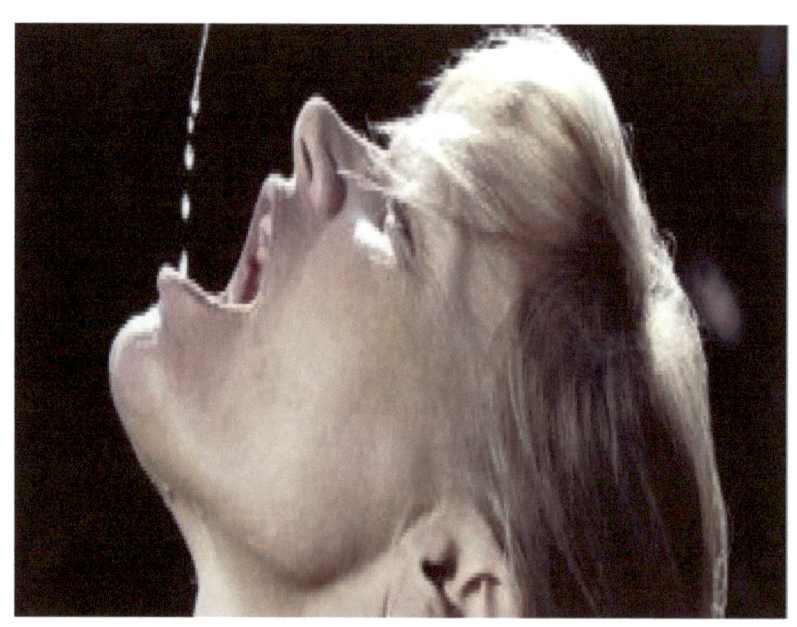

TWEET STORMS The Big Picture, Part 1

Yes, let your mind wander towards that glory that is her receiving mouth. She will love yours and hate all the others that came before . . .

5:57 PM · 23 October 2017

TWEET STORMS Pissing Contest @BombsAway

It says a lot about leaders so small
Who play war with words and our lives
They deserve eternity in a special hell
Filled with nuclear waste

7:40 PM - 9 October 2017

TWEET STORMS The Broken Windows
@PieceOfShit@MandalayBayHotel

Once shiny gold now empty black
I need room to rain on your parade
You won't find me in the dark
As you fight for your life
Your virtue dies

10:05-10:15 PM PDT · 1 October 2017

TWEET STORMS Puerto Rico
@TowelsForAll

A port so rich, now so wet
Drenched in anger and darkness
Water everywhere
Alas you are not a war zone
Clean up and fight
Fuerza en números

6:06 PM · 3 October 2017

TWEET STORMS The Blue And The Brown
@LatestFashionTrendGoneViral

Another day goes by
Another man in blue with brown shoes
And another, and another, and another
And . . . oh . . . this one is you
You fanboy

5:15 PM - 9 October 2017

TWEET STORMS — Take The Knee @ItAin'tAboutFootball

Go down and stay down
It will hurt worse if you don't
If they continue to kill for no reason
If they continue to disrespect
Change the game

7:55 PM · 9 October 2017

TWEET STORMS — **To Fallen Non-Friends**
@CouldHaveBeenMe

I have lost the count by now
Of all the shows I have seen
I blame age and fanaticism
One more Vegas, one too many
But the art heals wounds

5:05 PM · 9 October 2017

TWEET STORMS Intelligence Deficient
@MensaStrong

She would roll over in her box
My ex who was Mensa
She is spared your putrid ego
Those still mortal scream silently
Else the world goes deaf

5:20 PM - 12 October 2017

TWEET STORMS   **G.E.D.**   @Kingston5trong   

I admit it, it was always cottage country music to me. But your last stand was a display of courage. I long to possess such steadfast grace.

7:25 PM · 17 October 2017

TWEET STORMS — That Turning Point
@DownhillFromHere

When you are dealing more with people dying than with people birthing. Even those you never met yet made an impact are equally mourned.

6:37 PM - 23 October 2017

TWEET STORMS Rich Celebrity Rape Theory
@Weinstein+Trump=BirthControl

You make it soft for me
By making it hard for me
The nice guys lose because you believe
You deserve any pussy
You can even become president

2:45 PM · 13 October 2017

TWEET STORMS Thoughts and Prayers @NotEnough ⚙ *Following*

If actions speak louder than words, then why does society accept it when "leaders" give thoughts and prayers? Act your age . . . and act.

6:44 PM - 19 October 2017

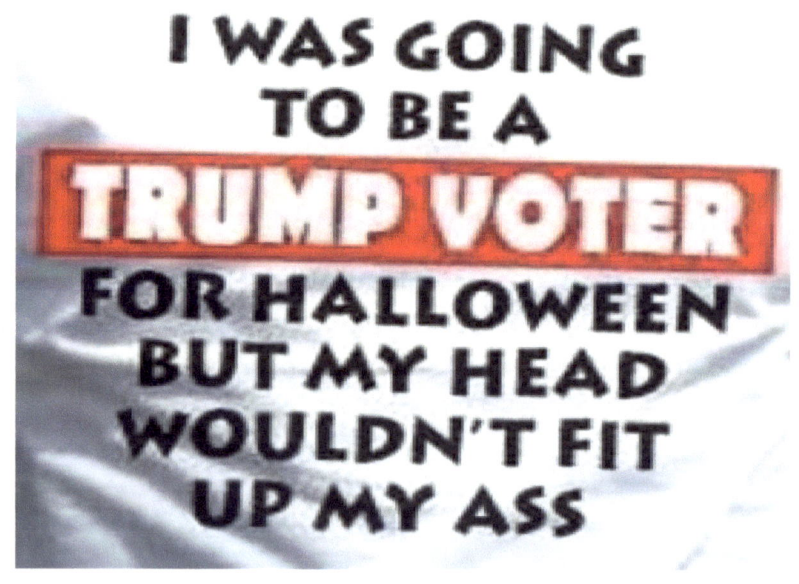

TWEET STORMS — Costume Party In Amurca
@SomewhereIKeepMyThoughtsToMyself   *Following*

On this colorful day
And three more times
Orange is really the new black
As the night darkens and ghosts emerge
Cheetos is the color I vote

11:59 PM - 31 October 2017

TWEET STORMS **Bonjour-Hi** @WeAllBelong ⚙ **Following**

"We have no business here": the companies who left or never came, the people who went away. Paranoia + racism: hope they pay your bills.

7:27 AM 8 December 2017

TWEET STORMS Sober Moral High Ground
@LeftHeavyDiamantePoem

Republican
Ambiguous-Employed
Kissing-Harassing-Groping
Roy Moore-Al Franken
Kissing-Harassing-Groping
Forthright-Unemployed
Democrat

6:22 PM - 11 December 2017

niggard

[nig-erd]

Word Origin

See more synonyms on Thesaurus.com

noun
1. an excessively parsimonious, miserly, or stingy person.

adjective
2. niggardly; miserly; stingy.

TWEET STORMS Niggard Is A Word
@Reallyitis

A ransom on your head if you dare utter it. The looks you may endure from a cheap bastard, even though you have really done nothing wrong.

7:25 PM - 24 December 2017

TWEET STORMS Blind Faith @NothingChanges

I heard my Boss in 1986 talk of blind faith
Simple enough to understand
How the years of curiosity have shown me
Lessons are not retained

7:13 PM - 24 December 2017

TWEET STORMS Live In Peace

Why do we hope for the dead to "rest in peace" when they are expired, yet you never hear people say "live in peace" to those that are alive?

12:45 PM · 28 November 2017

TWEET STORMS — Pay Your Way To Happiness
@TheRealThingIsFree

This capitalist life: with its shiny victories and short-lived joys, with its hollow kisses and golden toys. Here, where your freedom rises.

6:45 PM · 15 January 2018

TWEET STORMS The Big Picture, Part 2
@Here'sTheSoap

I will excerise and stay in shape, in order to run the extra mile required to beat the scum, and change the vision of their cum in my mouth.

6:05 PM · 23 October 2017

TWEET STORMS Reality's Helping Hand
@LogicIncorporated

You see that thing over there
Yeah, that thing you use for something
Science made that
Whatever that thing may be
Science made that
Not god

7:35 PM - 24 December 2017

TWEET STORMS SingleMinded
@WhoNeedsThemAnyways
Following

Inescapable desire for natural ego
Relentless drive for truth
Determined to succeed at life
Merciless happiness pursuer
Yet prefers albums?!

8:42 PM · 23 June 2018

TWEET STORMS #MeBecomingScaredToPraise
@WannaKeepMyJob

As a society, I hope we don't reach the point where no one is able to give even a simple compliment. Focus on the really Weinsteins please.

7:01 PM - 24 December 2017

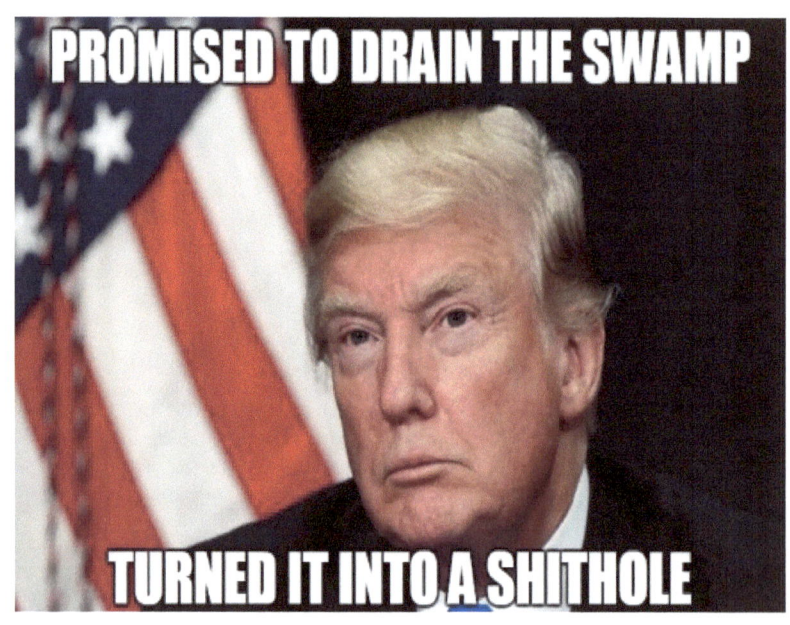

TWEET STORMS One Year In   @StillInTheWhiteHouse?!   Following

FUCK! FUCK! FUCK! FUCK! FUCK! FUCK!
FUCK! FUCK! FUCK! FUCK! FUCK! FUCK!
FUCK! FUCK! FUCKITY FUCK FUCK!
FUCK! FUCK! FUCK! FUCK! IMPEACH!!!!!!

1:00 PM - 20 January 2018

TWEET STORMS First In Everything ✦ Following
@TheGoldStandard?

Spotlight on they who finish first:
They get the recognition, the money, the gilded podium for their ego.
Show the rest of us how it's done.

1:21 PM · 14 April 2018

TWEET STORMS Kill All Double Standards
@InTheNameOfFairness

You want equality?
Then all double standards must go.
A male judge kissing a female contestant?
#MeTooed out & his career on life support.

11:33 PM - 11 March 2018

TWEET STORMS Defame & Scold For Profit
@StayOutOfMyKitchen

Fight against your abusers, they are always the weaker. Yet we watch abusive reality TV stars en masse, amused at the abuse they dish out.

6:45 PM - 14 March 2018

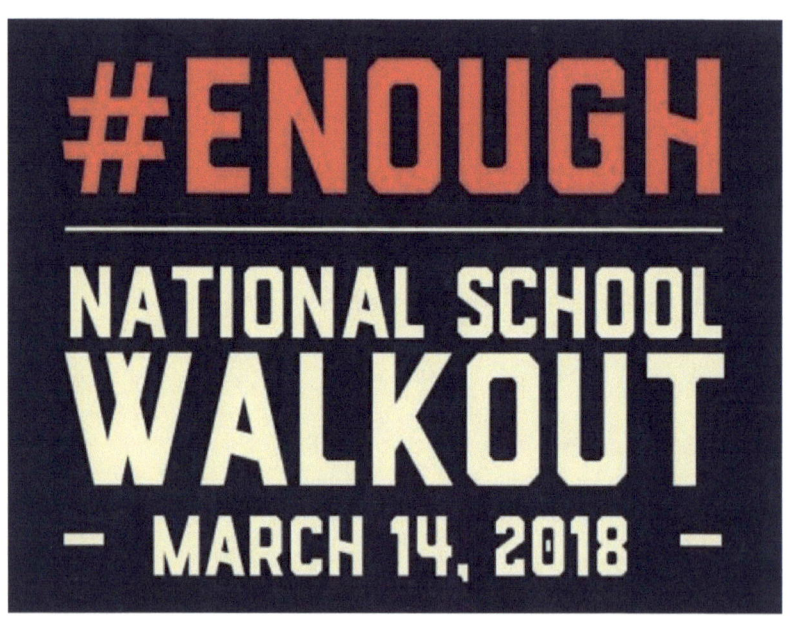

TWEET STORMS   Give Them The Brains, Not The Guns   
@NRA=Terrorism

Fight for me while I'm snug in the belly of my provider. Yet let me die while I try to make my living years better. Hypocrisy with a bullet.

6:30 PM - 14 March 2018

Donald J. Trump @realDonaldTrump · 4h
A perfectly executed strike last night. Thank you to France and the United Kingdom for their wisdom and the power of their fine Military. Could not have had a better result. Mission Accomplished!

💬 27K   ⟲ 26K   ♡ 106K

TWEET STORMS Distraction Warfare
@PeaceNeverAccomplished

Yes, we are stupid
You can play us for fools again
As you try and cling to life
Using that complex thing
Then again, a chemical attack hurts

10:00 PM - 13 April 2018

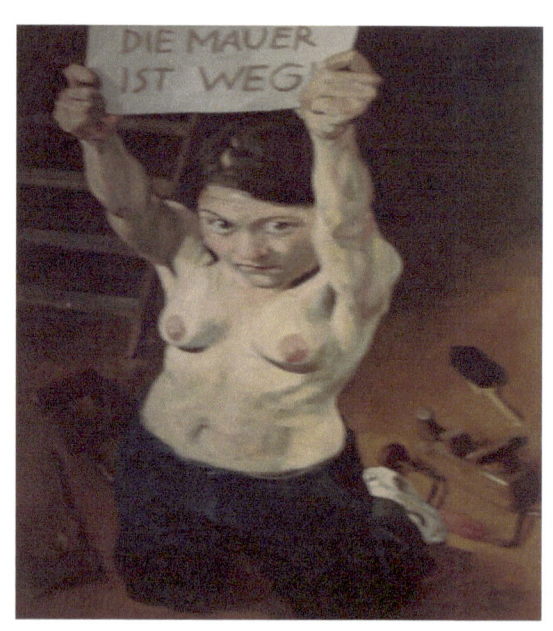

TWEET STORMS **Border Wall** @MexicoPays   Following

Tonight my bag is packed
I take this leap of faith to a better life
Or I dig my way to promised land
Stereotype all you want . . . I matter.

2:07 PM - 14 April 2018

TWEET STORMS LikeBlooded
@ISeeRed

 Following

The sameness of life:
Bringing despair and grief,
At times ennui and death.
And some things that are the same:
Easy like the human family.

7:48 PM · 8 January 2018

TWEET STORMS Justice Does Not Age @04/24/1915 Following

Advance and claim your place among humanity. The living have gone away now, without your violent aid. Generations of spineless politicians.

6:33 PM · 15 January 2018

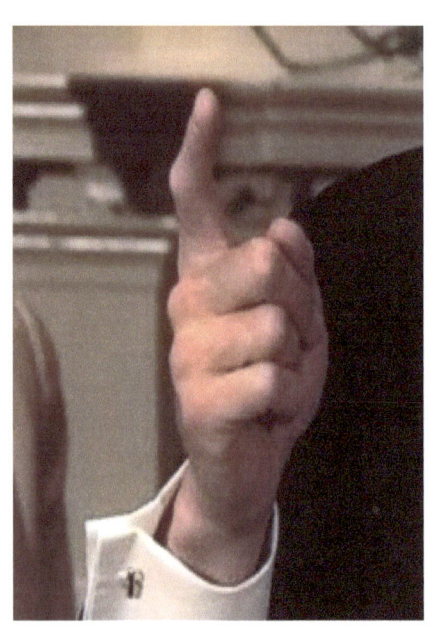

TWEET STORMS The 25th

What will it take to remove the stain?
Why all the talk, yet seemingly little action?
The other one was quite quick.
No oral sex this time.

5:15 PM - 14 October 2017

TWEET STORMS   **Restless Night**   @TroublesOnYourMind   

All evils come for you at night:
Social
Political
Emotional
Financial
Drumpfal
When do the wicked rest?
Allow us to live like mere normals?

10:16 PM - 23 June 2018

Life is a soup and i'm a fork

TWEET STORMS The Secrets Of Life @UphillFromHere

Wonder how things work
Wonder who you can turn to
Wonder when things will change
Wonder where things went wrong
Wonder what to do
Why then

8:30 PM - 9 May 2018

TWEET STORMS AntiSocial Media
@Let'sMeetUpAndNotChat

Can you sense what is close?
Can you feel what is tangible?
Are you willing to go that extra inch?
Lift your head up to me?
Thumbs at rest.

9:05 PM - 23 June 2018

TWEET STORMS Psycho The Rapist @NowLookingDownOnYou *Following*

Put it all together and that's what you need
You helped me grow
Helped me see equality
The closets of our lives
Filled to varying degrees

5:55 PM - 10 July 2018

TWEET STORMS Coat of Harms
@WrongTimeWrongPlace

What brings you here with words so odd?
A stand made falls down.
Words for hubby? The media? Maybe.
The caged children don't give a shit.

8:02 PM - 23 June 2018

TWEET STORMS **Entropy Monger** @WhartonSchoolOf(InsertVomitFaceEmoji)  Following

I start talking
Punch him in the face
Fake news
I won
Only the best people
More records that Elton
Pussy to grab
Put(a)in
What was I saying?

6:13 PM - 10 July 2018

TWEET STORMS Raving Nostomaniac — Following
@CastleSweetCastle

This unending slog
Brain stressed and tied up
You seek that place of rest
To warm your bones
To charm life's senses back from the dead

9:20 PM - 23 June 2018

OUTTWEETS

TWEET STORMS Haiku For Eric Stern
@R.I.P.

Guide us from afar
Leaving behind great challenge
For us to keep pace

7:43 PM · 26 February 2018

TWEET STORMS   **Cattitude** @LittleManOnyx   Following

A diamond from adopted rough
Still paining from your past
Live your feline years now in peace
We all require true love
Regardless of species

8:16 PM 23 June 2018

TWEET STORMS King Patrick
@BoyWonderOfNewfoundland

Think your own way
You'll truly succeed my love
Remember, I met you in Halifax
We were 4 waiting for my luggage
And your first show was KISS

8:08 AM NDT · 29 July 2010

AUTHOR'S NOTE

Dear Readers,

The origin of this, my second book, came about as my first book (*Son of a Beach*) was nearing completion in September 2017. I remember wanting a few more poems, and who should provide the inspiration you wonder? Your fearmongering leader of the Free World at the time, that's who.

Watching CNN one evening, coverage seemed to be exclusively on a flurry of tweets spewing from the brain of DJT. I clearly remember thinking to myself that there is nothing he seems to say or write that I do not understand; like I am listening/reading the rantings of a 10-year old (or younger).

From there, the inspirations for the poems "Psychu" and "#140" came to be. The former was a simple haiku, while for the latter, I used the Twitter guideline of no more than 140 characters to make my case. In the end I figured, if he can make such an impact using Twitter, then why not I?

As a compliment to "#140", I decided it might be neat to have an image meme to accompany the poem. I remembered a picture I had seen a while back: a close-up of his face with his right hand in the foreground, holding his thumb and index finger very close together. "A lot could fit in there given how he is" I thought to myself. So when *Son of a Beach* was published, the poem and image occupied a single page together, complementing each other quite nicely I thought.

And as I then continued to work on finalizing the first book, I realized that the idea for my second book was right in front of me: a collection of poems written as and looking like regular tweets, with accompanying images/photos/etc.

So in early October 2017, a full 3 months before the first book was even published, I started writing this one. As someone who had never wanted to use the real Twitter, I was reluctant to open an account solely for this purpose. Sure enough, the Internet of (many, many) Things provided me with a website where you could create authentic looking "fake" tweets.

And so you now hold in your hands these collected works from October 2017 to July 2018.

Whereas *Son of a Beach* was largely "inward looking" (at myself, my friends, and my own personal surroundings), I expressly wanted this one to be largely "outward looking": at the world I live in and the people, events and norms that shape it on an unending basis.

Most poems actually came about quickly, based on events that transpired during this period of time: the Vegas shootings, #MeToo, the Charlottesville riots, Take a Knee, the Parkland shootings, and of course plenty relating to Agent Orange, to name but a few. Other poems are just me attempting to lay bare my core beliefs, on such things as: racism, sexism, religion, social media, abuse, fashion trends . . . you know, all the important stuff you find out about "along the way".

And if you were wondering, the answer is "Yes": I do know that Twitter now allows for 280 characters per tweet. However, I did want to challenge myself with fewer characters to work with, not to mention keeping it "Old School".

And with that, thank you very much for showing interest in my second book. I hope it will not be the last. As I stated in the first one: "We'll see what life brings won't we!"

Michael Bournazian
September 15, 2018

www.ingramcontent.com/pod-product-compliance
Lightning Source LLC
Chambersburg PA
CBHW041609220426
43667CB00001B/14